Taylor Swift FOR PIANO SOLO

ISBN 978-1-4584-1966-8

HAL•LEONARD®
CORPORATION

7777 W. BLUEMOUND RD. P.O. BOX 13819 MILWAUKEE, WI 53213

Visit Hal Leonard Online at
www.halleonard.com

BACK TO DECEMBER

Words and Music by
TAYLOR SWIFT

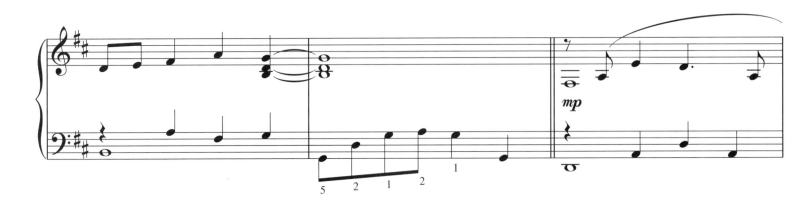

FIFTEEN

Words and Music by
TAYLOR SWIFT

To Coda ⊕

D.S. al Coda

CODA

FEARLESS

Words and Music by TAYLOR SWIFT,
LIZ ROSE and HILLARY LINDSEY

Moderately

LOVE STORY

Words and Music by
TAYLOR SWIFT

Moderately

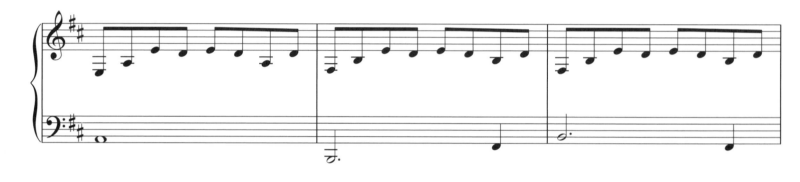

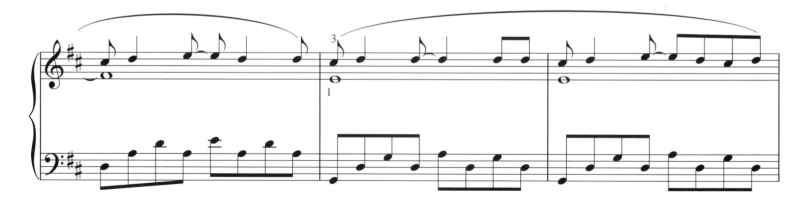

MEAN

Words and Music by
TAYLOR SWIFT

Moderately fast

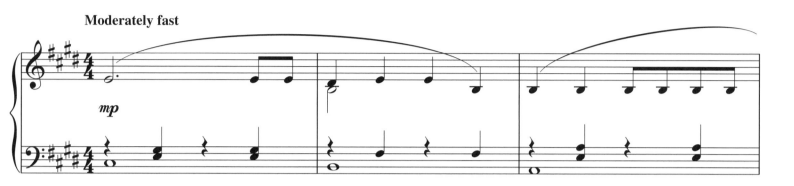

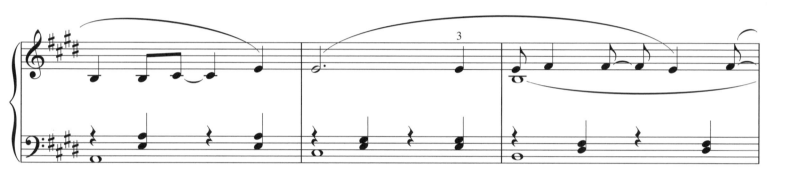

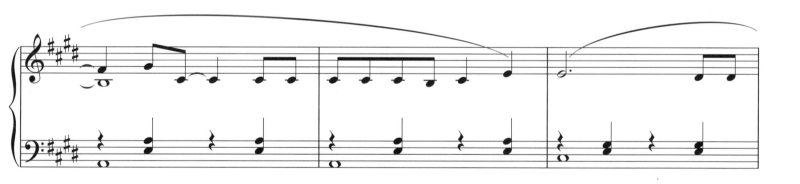

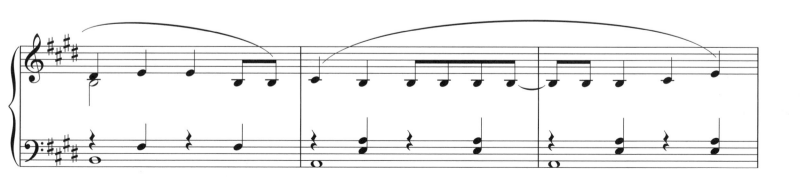

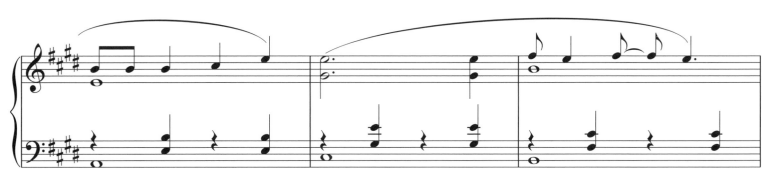

D.S. al Coda

CODA

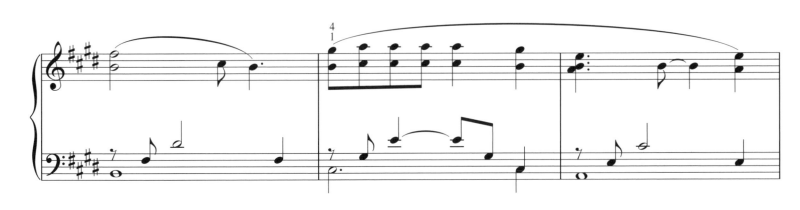

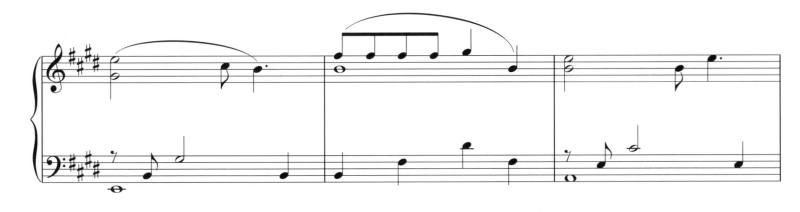

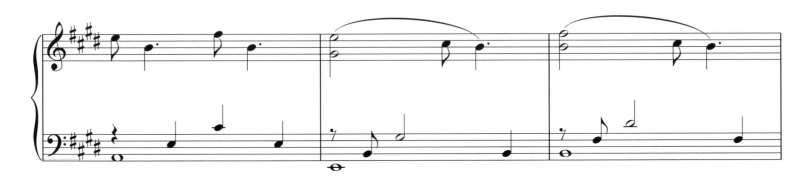

MINE

Words and Music by
TAYLOR SWIFT

Moderately fast

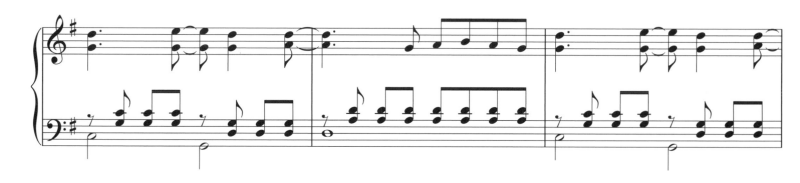

OUR SONG

Words and Music by
TAYLOR SWIFT

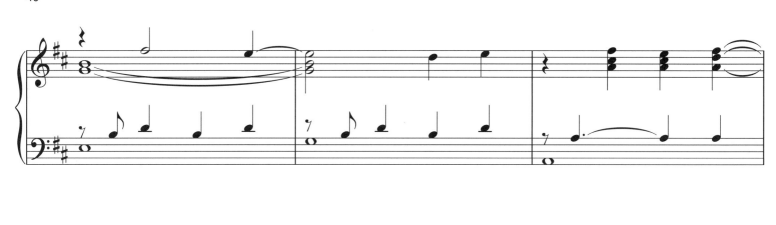

SPARKS FLY

Words and Music by
TAYLOR SWIFT

To Coda ⊕

PICTURE TO BURN

Words and Music by TAYLOR SWIFT
and LIZ ROSE

SHOULD'VE SAID NO

Words and Music by
TAYLOR SWIFT

SPEAK NOW

Words and Music by
TAYLOR SWIFT

WHITE HORSE

Words and Music by TAYLOR SWIFT
and LIZ ROSE

THE STORY OF US

Words and Music by
TAYLOR SWIFT

With energy

TEARDROPS ON MY GUITAR

Words and Music by TAYLOR SWIFT
and LIZ ROSE

To Coda

YOU BELONG WITH ME

Words and Music by TAYLOR SWIFT
and LIZ ROSE